SHREWSBURY

A Portrait in Old Picture Postcards

by

Sheila Hart

Foreword
by
Dr. Barrie Trinder

S. B. Publications

First published in 1988 by S. B. Publications

Unit 2, The Old Station Yard, Pipe Gate, Market Drayton, Shropshire TF9 4HY

Reprinted 1991

ISBN 1 870708 11 3

Printed in Great Britain by Stowes the Printers, Longton, Stoke-on-Trent, Staffordshire ST3 2PT

CONTENTS

Page

CONTENTS

CONTENTS

FOREWORD
by
Dr. Barrie Trinder

Since about 1960 we have come to think of the picture postcard as a work of art, dreaming spires soaring above misty meadows, or alternatively as a particularly tasteless form of souvenir, five views of Scarborough wrapped up in the entrails of a tortoise. Picture postcards of earlier years are rather different, often showing the most mundane scenes in places far from the accustomed trails of tourists. For that reason the postcard is increasingly valued as an historical source.

Sheila Hart's new selection of postcards of Shrewsbury demonstrates how postcard publishers were aiming to sell their products to people whose everyday surroundings were pictured upon them, rather than to tourists. It also shows how useful the postcard can be to the local historian. We see parts of the town which have totally changed, like Hill's Lane, St. Alkmund's Square and Meole Brace before the bypass. We see people at work, like the tailors employed by John Kerry. We sense something of the tastes of past times, like the inter-war fashion for cosy cafés. We see chain stores encroaching on the shopping streets. This book makes available a valuable source for the study of Shrewsbury's past and local historians will have cause to be grateful for it.

Dr. Barrie Trinder
Ironbridge Institute

INTRODUCTION

The first pictures on postcards in this country were published in 1894. These early picture cards were known as "Court Cards", smaller in size than the standard cards of today, with the address on one side and the illustration and correspondence on the other. The standard size of picture postcard was introduced in the early 20th. century - on this the illustration occupied the whole of one side, whilst the message and address went on the reverse. Gradually, picture postcard collecting became a national craze and almost every household could boast of an album of cards for visitors to see and admire. Millions of postcards were printed and posted annually encouraged by the ½d postage rate and this vast output of postcards depicted every subject imaginable. The era to 1914 is referred to as the "Golden Age of Postcards" after which the use of the postcard went into gradual decline. This was caused mainly by the increased use of the telephone and the rise in postal rates. Fine collections were to lie dormant and forgotten for many years and only during the last twenty years have they been re-discovered. Today picture postcard collecting is a very popular pastime.

Topographical cards are much sought by today's collectors who look for nostalgic memories of days gone by. Cards of Shrewsbury are no exception and are always in demand, especially the photographic examples of the town.

During the "Golden Age" there were numerous national and local publishers of postcards. Probably the most prolific of Shrewsbury's local publishers were Wildings of Shrewsbury who recorded life in the town and county, and many examples of their work are included in this book.

The picture postcard is often the sole source of visual material about towns, villages, industries, fashion, transport and events from years past. Postcards should never be discarded or damaged but should be carefully stored, or offered to collectors, dealers, local museums or libraries.

INTRODUCTION

So many excellent books and booklets have been published about Shrewsbury, that it was a rather daunting experience to compile yet another. The aim of this book is to provide further visual material on the changes experienced by the town and its environs. With the exception of page 99, all the views are on picture postcards, the majority selected from my own collection of Shrewsbury and Shropshire to which I add whenever possible.

If the date beneath a card is printed as "circa", then I have used directories to try to ensure relative accuracy, otherwise the date is on the reverse of the card, either in the message or postmark.

I have enjoyed the challenge of producing this book, and I trust that it may revive happy memories and give pleasure to those who recall Shrewsbury's "Good Old Days".

Sheila Hart
Shrewsbury

THE COAT OF ARMS OF SHREWSBURY

The Coat of Arms of Shrewsbury illustrated by a postcard published by Stoddart & Co. of Halifax in their 'Ja-Ja' heraldic series, which covered almost every city and town in the British Isles.

The Arms comprise of three leopards' heads in gold on a blue shield. Controversy still surrounds the origin of the leopards' heads, or 'loggerheads', which appeared on the Corporation's Seal during the fifteenth century.

The Latin motto "Floreat Salopia" means "May Salop Flourish".

THE SQUARE, 1924
The central features of The Square are the Old Market Hall, built c. 1596,
and the statue of Clive of India erected in 1860.
For many years buses commenced their journeys from The Square. The Midland bus shown here
serviced the route to Cruckton, Yockleton, Westbury and Worthen. Behind the bus, the shelter
had previously been used by hansom-cab drivers. The timber-framed frontage belongs to
The Plough public house and to the right, behind Clive's statue, was Grocott's shop.

2

THE SQUARE, c. 1905
The Shire Hall was designed by Sir Robert Smirke and built in 1836-7.
It stood on the corner of The Square and High Street until c.1970, when it was demolished
to be replaced by modern offices and shops.
The interior suffered damage from a fire in 1881 resulting in considerable alteration.
The main entrance was further altered in 1954.
Notice the hansom-cab parked behind Clive's statue.

THE SQUARE, c. 1910

The Salop Old Bank (Capital and Counties Bank) was on the opposite corner from the Shire Hall.
Later the premises became incorporated into Grocott's drapery stores.
Like the Shire Hall, the bank was an elegant and dignified building

THE MUSIC HALL, THE SQUARE, 1908
The Music Hall, built in 1840, occupies part of the site of Vaughan's Mansion.
In 1906, the Music Hall was described as "the only Hall in the town of sufficient size and convenience for Concerts, Entertainments and Public Meetings. Holding nearly 1000 people, brilliantly lighted, with a raised orchestra the full width of the Hall, and acoustic properties unsurpassed for musical effect".

THE SQUARE, 1920

The Missionary Festival was held in Shrewsbury on 26th June, 1920. It was attended by
6 Bishops, a Dean, 3 Archdeacons, 90 clergy and 350 choristers and led by the Bishop of Lichfield.
The procession traversed much of the town.
This postcard, shows the procession in front of the Shire Hall, after having been
addressed by the Mayor. During the Missionary Festival, addresses were given
in various churches throughout the town.

THE SQUARE, c. 1910
Looking across the end of The Square to Princess Street,
with the Old Market Hall and its sundial (still there) prominent in the foreground.
The timbered property on the corner was Lloyd's Mansion, built in the 16th century
and approximately the same age as the Market Hall.
The Mansion, which later became part of Della Porta's store, was demolished when the Shire Hall
was extended. The site is now occupied by Princess House.

MARKET STREET, 1907
A well-remembered shop, in
business over many years, at 13
Market Street.
Outside stand the owner, Mr.
McEwan Davies, and his wife,
in front of a superb display of
hardware, earthenware and china.
Inside, towards the back of the shop,
was a book department.

MARKET STREET, c. 1912

The County Restaurant, owned by the Shrewsbury Café Company Ltd.,
stood on the corner of Market Street and Swan Hill.
This advertising postcard shows one of the dining rooms, which was part of the spacious
dining, coffee and smoke rooms on the premises.
The back of the postcard has been used to advertise for a waitress who
"must be tall and of good appearance".

PRINCESS STREET, c. 1906
Looking along Princess Street to The
Square with the Old Market Hall
and shop frontages beyond.
The various and somewhat
dilapidated buildings which made
up part of Della Porta's premises
are on the immediate right - these
extended from the corner
to No. 5, Princess Street and through
to High Street.

HIGH STREET, 1906
A busy view along High Street towards Mardol Head.
The women wear the fashions of the day, and only horse transport occupies the roadway.
On the right is the entrace to Grope Lane. The shops in the right foreground include:
Edwin Murrell, seedsman and nurseryman; T. Golding, hatter and hosier; and beyond, H. Wells, antique dealer.
On the left, in the background, are the Salop Old Bank with Ireland's Mansion beyond.

HIGH STREET, c. 1930
Photographed from near the junction with Mardol Head and looking up High Street
towards Shearman's Hall at the end of Milk Street.
In the foreground, Owen's Mansion dates back to c. 1592 and was originally the home of Richard Owen,
a wool merchant. At the time of this photograph, the building was occupied by
Maddox & Co. Ltd., drapers and outfitters.
In the centre, the tall building with the multi-shaped gable was built in 1892 and designed by
A. Lloyd Oswell. On the right is part of the Shire Hall.

THE UNITARIAN CHURCH, HIGH STREET

The Unitarian Church was founded in Shrewsbury in the 17th century after there had been
religious strife in the town resulting from the Act of Uniformity.
The building was destroyed by a mob in 1715 but later rebuilt by public subscription in 1839-40
and further enlarged in 1884-85.
It contains a monument to Charles Darwin who died in 1882.

IRELAND'S MANSION, HIGH STREET, c. 1929

Ireland's Mansion, a magnificent timber-framed house, was built in the late 16th century by Robert Ireland, a wool merchant. Its frontage is one of the finest in Shrewsbury, with its three storeys, surmounted by dormer windows. In this view, Grocott's, outfitters and drapers, occupied the premises of the former Salop Old Bank.

MILK STREET, c. 1929
A view through the archway into the
courtyard of the Old Post Office
Hotel; part of which is a
16th-century house built by George
Proud, a Shrewsbury draper. The
house fronts on to Milk Street.
The inn is behind the archway and
was used by many Shropshire
carriers in the 19th century.

ST. JULIAN'S CHURCH, FISH STREET, 1929

St. Julian's Church was almost entirely rebuilt in 1749-50 on the site of an early 13th-century church. The south front was altered in 1846 and the church was further enlarged and restored in 1883. The tower, shown here during restoration work in 1929, was built above its original base (c. 1200) and held six bells. St. Julian's Church is now used as a craft centre. On the left can be seen part of the 184 ft. spire of St. Alkmund's Church, and part of Bagnall & Brown, grocers.

ST. JULIAN'S CHURCH, c. 1920
Many will recall the times when they attended services within this church.
It was one of four parish churches sited in close proximity in central Shrewsbury.
After being enlarged in 1883, it could seat a congregation of 500.
Much of its former beauty is still visible when one visits the craft centre.

FISH STREET, c. 1925
Unlike most of the central streets
of Shrewsbury,
Fish Street was a street of
small cottage-type buildings
varying in style.
On the immediate left are the
buildings which featured in the Bear
Steps renovation scheme.

BUTCHER ROW, c. 1910
The street-level windows of the late
15th-century Abbot's House formed
individual shops in medieval times.
They were open to the street during
the day, but shuttered at night;
part of the shuttering possibly
forming the counters
during trading hours.
The projecting first floor would have
given some protection from bad
weather or hot sun.

BUTCHER ROW, c. 1929
Looking along Butcher Row
towards the spire of
St. Alkmund's Church
with the Abbot's House on the right,
on the corner of Fish Street.
The property facing the camera,
occupied at this time by the firm of
J. Blower, was demolished
in the 1960s.

ST. ALKMUND'S SQUARE,
c. 1910

St. Alkmund's Vicarage was built in
the 19th century and later served as
the Vicarage for St. Julian's Church.
In the mid-19th century it was the
home of Mrs. Julia Wightman who
campaigned for teetotalism.
Also she founded the Working Men's
Hall in the Square,
and organised evening Bible classes
in the town.
Mrs. Wightman, who became a very
respected lady, died in 1898.

WYLE COP, c. 1922

Showing how narrow Wyle Cop used to be, prior to the demolition of the property on the corner of Dogpole and the re-alignment of the buildings on the left-hand side. The corner property, advertising McEwan's Scotch Ales, was the London House Inn, formerly the London Coffee House.

In the right foreground can be seen the entrance to the former Juvenile Employment Bureau, and next door, R. H. Stawart, tobacconist. In the centre is the Lion Hotel, which dates back to the 15th century and which was rebuilt in the 18th and 19th centuries. The lion, above the porch, was erected in 1777. Adjoining the Lion Hotel is the Henry Tudor House built in the early 15th century. Note the traffic mirror and the A49 road sign near the Lion Hotel.

WYLE COP
Although postally used in 1926, this postcard shows the 'top of the Cop' in c. 1919,
before the road was widened and the shop-fronts on the left were demolished
to be replaced by new shops sited further back.
The sign on the left advertises Evans and Brown, jewellers and watchmakers, who had
"an establishment replete with all modern appliances
for the execution of watch and clock repairs in a skilful manner".

WYLE COP, c. 1919

This card shows the bottom of Wyle Cop leading on to the steep, narrow old English Bridge.
The Hero of Moultan Inn (on the left) was named in honour of Sir H. B. Edwardes of Frodesley
who gained fame through his bravery during the Second Sikh War (1848-1849).
Horses with carts, traps or carriages, formed the chief means of transport at this time.

WYLE COP, 1933
A good example of how picture postcards record social history.
The photograph shows the change of use of the former 'Hero of Moultan Inn', which was de-
licensed in 1924, and later occupied by:
The Sherar Tea Rooms; E. A. Lewis, watch and clock maker; and A. G. Page, family grocer.
The Sherar Tea Rooms were named after Thomas Sherar who lived in these buildings,
known as Sherar's Mansion, in 1573. Notice the line of the English Bridge, widened in 1926.

TOWN WALLS, 1910

Looking across Town Walls to the Roman Catholic Cathedral which was designed by
Edward Pugin and built in 1856 at the expense of the Earl of Shrewsbury.
Behind the Cathedral are the rear extensions of the houses in Belmont
which contains many elegant properties built mainly in the 18th century.

TOWN WALLS, c. 1910
The Town Walls, which once
enclosed most of Shrewsbury,
were started c. 1226,
during the reign of Henry III, and
completed some thirty years later.
At one time there were 12 towers
similar to the Old Watch Tower,
now the only remaining example
and donated to the National Trust.
Notice the restored battlements.
Beyond the tower is the former
Ebenezer Chapel, erected by the
Methodist New Connexion in 1834,
now used by the Shrewsbury High
School.

TOWN WALLS, c. 1925
Swan Hill Court House is an imposing residence standing in its own grounds behind ornate iron gates.
This magnificent Georgian House was designed by Thomas Pritchard and built in 1761
as the residence for the Marquis of Bath.
It was later occupied by the Duke of Cleveland.

MURIVANCE, c. 1910
The Eye, Ear and Throat Hospital, designed by C. O. Ellison of Liverpool
and built between 1879 and 1881, was funded by voluntary subscription.
The entrance to the hospital was from the toll road leading over Kingsland Bridge,
shown in the left background built in 1883.
The tollgates, toll-keeper's hut, and the roof of the toll-keeper's cottage can be seen on the extreme left.

ST. CHAD'S TERRACE, 1910

Gifts of money from the Shropshire Horticultural Society have done much to enhance the town. Two examples of their generosity are the wall along St. Chad's Terrace, built in 1906, and Quarry Lodge, built in 1886, shown on the postcard just beyond St. Chad's Church.

On the left is the War Memorial dedicated to the men of the King's Shropshire Light Infantry who died in the Boer War. The memorial was unveiled in 1902.

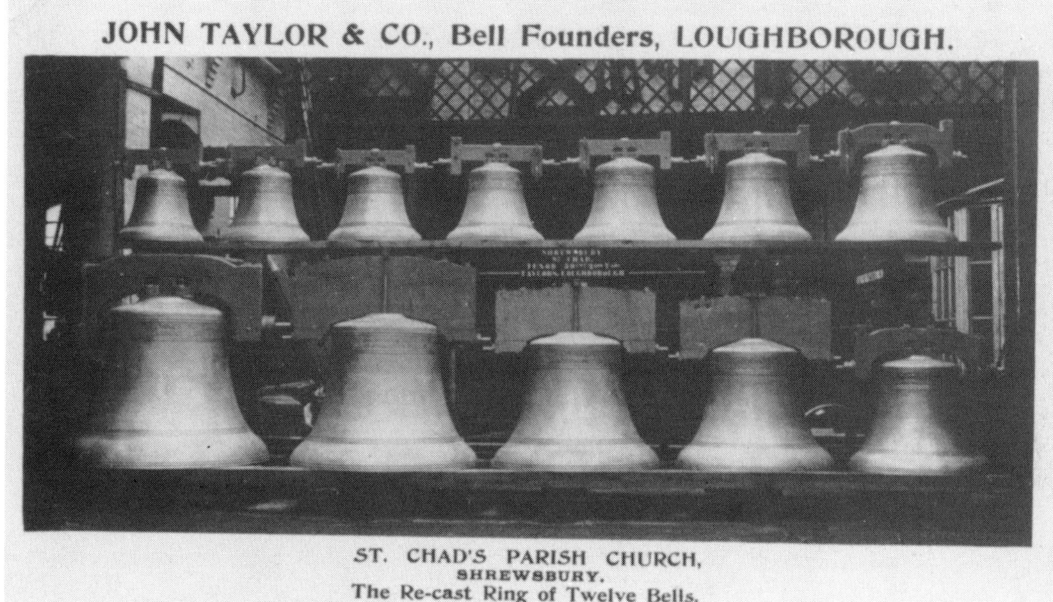

ST. CHAD'S CHURCH, 1914

The original ring of twelve bells for St. Chad's Church were cast in 1798,
after the church had been built in 1790-92.
This postcard shows the ring of bells after they were re-cast and re-hung by Taylors of
Loughborough; a town famous for its bell-foundry. The twelve bells were re-dedicated in May
1914.
The tenor bell, weighing almost two tons, is 16½ feet in circumference and roughly the same
height as an average man. A thirteenth bell has been added recently.
(see also page 34)

THE QUARRY, 1922

The Shropshire War Memorial stands in Quarry Avenue close to St. Chad's Church.
The memorial consists of an open rotunda, designed by George Hubbard & Son, under which
stands a bronze statue of St.Michael with a lance in his left hand and his right hand extended in blessing.
The memorial was unveiled by the Earl of Powis on 29th July, 1922.
The guard of honour was provided by the men of the King's Shropshire Light Infantry and the
Royal Air Force. 200 choristers from local churches attended the ceremony.

THE QUARRY, c. 1920
The felling of the stately lines of lime
trees in The Quarry in the late 1940s
caused a furore in the town.
Many of the trees had been planted
to commemorate
Queen Victoria's Diamond Jubilee,
but in 1948 they were deemed
to be unsafe.
By 1950, new trees had been planted
under the direction
of the late Percy Thrower.

THE QUARRY, 1906
The musical rides, bands, fireworks, and other spectacles
have always been popular features of the Shrewsbury Flower Show.
In 1906, at the Shrewsbury Floral Fête, one of the major attractions
was 'The Great Caicedo' - King of the Wire. This breathtaking act consisted of somersaults and
pirouettes on a wire stretched 40 feet above the ground.
In the background is St. Chad's Church designed by George Steuart.

THE QUARRY, 1905
Balloon flights have long been a
feature at the Flower Show, or
Floral Fête as it was first called.
Many of the early flights at the Fête
were "piloted" by Messrs. A. and P.
Spencer who usually took three
ballons to the show.
The postcard shows one of the
balloons ascending above the
Flower Show, after having been
released from its restraining weights.

THE PRIORY, 1910

The Jubilee Baths were built in 1894 at a cost of £7000 and contained two swimming and ten slipper baths. Earlier Baths, opened in 1832, had a swimming bath, hot baths, vapour baths & hot air, sulphurous & medicated baths. If there were cases of cholera, the portable baths could be "hired free of charge and used at the patient's house".

SWAN HILL, 1911
The Old Porch House, built in 1628,
takes its name from a timber porch,
which once protected its entrance.
The porch was removed possibly
because it obstructed traffic.
The letters above the door relate to
Thomas Ridley, probably the 17th
century builder and first owner.
It is said to contain a secret hiding
place, which could well have been
used in times of religious
persecution.

OLD PORCH HOUSE, SHREWSBURY—1628.

ST. JOHN'S HILL, c. 1929
Looking down St. John's Hill towards Shoplatch and Pride Hill in the distance. On the left, the Methodist Chapel was built in 1805 and rebuilt in 1879. Further down, under the lamp and above the blind, the sign reads Dolphin Pawnbrokers. On the right, the shops include (from right to left): Livesey's;
E. Gregory, newsagent;
J. W. Powell, confectioner.
The tall building in the right background was the Theatre Royal. In the centre of the picture is the imposing Victorian Market Hall with its 151 ft. tower, designed by Griffiths of Stafford and built in 1867-9.

BRIDGE STREET, c. 1900

St. Chad's Church was built in 1838 by E. Haycock as a school for the education of the poor in the parish of St. Chad. Initially it provided a day school for 160 boys and also a Sunday school. An infant's school was added in 1865. The schools were demolished when Bridge Street was widened, and part of the site is now occupied by the multi-storey car park at the upper end of Barker Street.

BARKER STREET, c. 1935
Rowley's House, a superb example of a timber-framed and plaster house, was built in the 16th century and occupied by Roger Rowley, draper, brewer and maltster. His son built Rowley's Mansion, shown on the left, c. 1618 - the earliest brick mansion in Shrewsbury.
Both buildings have been extensively restored and Rowley's House is used as a museum by the Borough Council, housing a magnificent collection of material excavated from the Roman city of Uriconium.

HILL'S LANE, c. 1920
Hill's Lane was named after John
Hill, Mayor of Shrewsbury in 1689,
who lived in Rowley's Mansion
during the 17th century.
The postcard view shows Rowley's
Mansion and the adjoining New Ship
Inn; both buildings in a dilapidated
state of repair. The inn, along with
much of Barker Street, was
demolished during slum clearance
and road widening during the 1930s.
Rowley's Mansion once the Vicarage
of St. Chad's Church, also a
warehouse, was left derelict for
many years until major work
restored it to its present state.

Hill's Lane - Shrewsbury.

HILL'S LANE, c. 1909
Showing a very different Hill's Lane
from today. Many of the buildings
shown have been demolished to be
replaced
by the bus station.
The Old Gullet Inn, shown on the
left, was the meeting place for the
prestigious Gullet Club, whose
members included many influential
men of town and county.
The Old Gullet Inn was de-licensed
c. 1941.

MARDOL, c. 1920
Photographed by the old Market Hall and looking down the busy thoroughfare of Mardol.
This was once the main route out of Shrewsbury via the Welsh Bridge. Mardol was part of a
densely populated area at the turn of the century, having many shops, industries
and at least eight public houses.
The shops in view include the following: On the left, Eastmans Ltd. and Southern Bros. On the
right, Briggs & Co., boots and shoes; The London Central Meat Co. Ltd., and centre right, Brown & Sons.

MARDOL, c. 1909
A second view of Mardol, photographed further down the street looking towards the
15th-century King's Head Inn in the far distance.
Mardol was very much a 'shopping street' including butchers' shops.
On the left, the shops include: James Davies, butchers; and Dick's (Robert & James), bootmakers.
On the right, the business belonged to R. D. Bromley, corn merchant.

SMITHFIELD ROAD, c. 1950

During the 19th century, the yard of the Britannia Hotel was the starting place for coaches, carriers and stage waggons to north and mid-Wales.
Later, at the turn of the century, several country bus services also started from here.
Until c. 1820, the Britannia was formerly known as The Welsh Harp, and in 1987, the Britannia changed its name to The Shrewsbury.
The junction with Mardol can be seen on the left.

PRIDE HILL, c. 1912

It is thought that Pride Hill was named after a family who owned shops and a house there early in the 13th century.

The upper storeys of the buildings lining Pride Hill may seem to be little changed, but at street level things are different. The shops sold a much wider variety of goods ranging from fish, groceries, fruit, general ironmongery, to clothing and footwear.

The tower of the old Market Hall can be seen in the background.

7, PRIDE HILL, c. 1902
Gone are the days when one could shop at Boots the Chemists,
and then visit their Charming Café located upstairs.
The café accommodated 200 people and also provided a Ladies' Room and Smoke Room.
Boots advertised "Luxury with Economy, High-Class Luncheons and Teas at Popular Prices".

PRIDE HILL, c. 1902

Shrewsbury Head Post Office, an impressive Victorian gothic-styled building, dating from 1877, stood on the corner of Pride Hill and St. Mary's Street. Its main entrance can be seen behind the street lamp. The building was demolished in the early 1960s and the new Head Post Office, built in 1966, is now located in St. Mary's Street.

On the left, beyond the Post Office, can be seen part of the Drapers' Almshouses which were rebuilt in 1825. On the extreme right is part of the Clarendon Hotel.

Raven Hotel, Shrewsbury

Telephone : Shrewsbury 476 & 477
Telegrams : Raven Hotel, Shrewsbury

CASTLE STREET, c. 1923

During the 18th century, Castle Street was known as High Pavements, also as Raven Street after
the Raven Inn which had been in existence since the late 16th century and had become one of
Shrewsbury's famous coaching inns.
The street was formally adopted as Castle Street. c. 1850
This advertising postcard for the Raven Hotel, built on the site of the Raven Inn in the late 19th century,
shows a large crowd gathered to watch the hunt assemble outside the main entrance.

CASTLE STREET, c. 1940
An advertising postcard published by Honywood Hotels, the owners of the Raven Hotel.
The 'Raven' was a popular commercial and family hotel and provided transport for its guests by
horse and carriage, in later years by car, to and from the station.
In 1959, the Raven Hotel closed and was demolished a year later.
The entire contents of the hotel were auctioned over six days in February 1960.

CASTLE STREET, 1922
Plimmer's Bakery, confectionery shop and Castle Restaurant stood on the corner of School Lane.
Earlier, these premises had been known as Pailin's Cake Shop.
From the many and varied advertisements outside the bakery, Plimmer's claimed
to continue to bake Pailin's Shrewsbury Cakes from the original recipe.

SCHOOL LANE, c. 1900
An artistic impression of School
Lane showing the former Royal
Free Grammar School.
When the school moved to
Kingsland, this building was
purchased from the school
governors and opened as a public
library in April 1885.

CASTLE STREET, c. 1920
Looking down Castle Street towards
the former Presbyterian Church of
St. Nicholas, built in 1870
and closed in 1975.
Beyond the Church is Castle Gates
House, a splendid timber-framed
building which formerly stood in
Dogpole. The house was dismantled
and re-erected in Castle Street in
1696 by the Newport family (The
Earls of Bradford).

SALOPIA NEVER FORGETS   C. W. Lloyd Copyright

'SALOPIA NEVER FORGETS'

During the morning of 5th August, 1919, a wreath-laying ceremony was held
at a specially constructed cenotaph, sited on the lawn outside the Library, in memory of the men
who had lost their lives during World War I.
In the right background, the bronze statue to Charles Darwin, the famous naturalist and former
pupil of Shrewsbury School, was sculptured by H. Montford and erected in 1897.

CASTLE STREET, c. 1909

A glimpse of Castle Street through the opening beneath the Council House Gatehouse.
This timber-framed building dates from 1620 and is reputed to have been used as a prison by the Court of the Marches.
The Old Council House was built in 1502 with restoration and alterations made in the 18th century. It was used by the Council of the Welsh Marches for its meetings, and both Charles I and James II stayed there.

THE CASTLE, c. 1910
A more unusual view of the Library tower seen through one of the doorways in the Castle. The roof and chimney belong to a building in Castle Street, well below the Castle Wall.
Shrewsbury Castle was built by Roger de Montgomery in 1083, with major building work completed during the reign of Henry II and Edward I. In 1790, the Castle was converted into a private residence for Sir William Pulteney by Thomas Telford, the engineer. In 1924, the Castle was bought by the Shropshire Horticultural Society and presented to the town. It is now the Shropshire Regimental Museum housing the collections of the King's Shropshire Light Infantry, The Shropshire Yeomanry Cavalry and the Shropshire Royal Horse Artillery.

THE CASTLE, 1910

On Monday, 8th May 1910, the accession of King George V was officially proclaimed throughout various parts of the town by Mr. B. Blower, Mayor of Shrewsbury.
The proclamation was read out in The Square, on Wyle Cop, on St. Chad's Terrace, at the Butter Cross and at the Castle, as shown on this postcard.
Shropshire Regimental troops, Shrewsbury School's Cadet Corps and the Band of the Shropshire Yeomanry were in attendance for the ceremony.

THE CASTLE, c. 1910

The main point of interest in this rooftop view of the town is the water tower which stood in the
space bounded by St. Mary's Street, Butcher Row and Pride Hill.
Prior to the mid-19th century, unfiltered water was pumped up from the river with the ever-
present risk of disease, and very often the supply was inadequate for the town's domestic needs.
To overcome this problem, a huge circular tank with a capacity of 250,000 gallons, was designed
by Tisdale and constructed in 1860, so providing the town with a supply of water, which,
in times of drought, was often inadequate.

CASTLE GATES, 1909

The Station Hotel (not the official station hotel) stood on Castle Gates next to Baker's, the boot shop, on Meadow Place corner.
It was used frequently by North Shropshire carriers from the 1880s until the early 1900s. Baker's shop and the hotel were demolished in 1935 to make way for the Granada Theatre. Later the theatre became a cinema, and in 1973 it was converted into a bingo hall.

THE RAILWAY STATION, c. 1906
The original Station on this site in Shrewsbury was built by Thomas Brassey and designed by
T. Penson, Jnr. It was opened on 12th October, 1848 and served the Shrewsbury and Chester Railway.
At the turn of the century major alterations were undertaken to enlarge the station which
included the excavation of a new ground floor beneath the original building - explaining why one
has to climb steps to platform level.
In the foreground, workmen can be seen finishing work on the shelter for hansom-cab drivers.

AERIAL VIEW OF SHREWSBURY

The aerial view, probably photographed in the early 1920s, shows Castle Gates, the Library, the Castle, the Council House, the Prison, and the Station. The view is particularly interesting and illustrates the extent of the vast overall roof which extended onto the railway bridge over the river. The roof was constructed when the station was enlarged at the turn of the century, but much of it was dismantled in 1924.

CHESTER STREET, 1922
The Greyhound Hotel, formerly The Masons' Arms up until 1879, stood at 1, Chester Street.
For a time, the hotel displayed a sign, painted by Edwin Cole, depicting the famous greyhound named Master McGrath, winner of the Waterloo Cup in 1868, 1869 and 1871.
The Greyhound Hotel was demolished in 1939 when road widening took place.

CHESTER STREET, 1912
John Kerry, a gentlemen's outfitter, tailor, hosier and glover, occupied the premises at 2, 3 and 4,
Chester Street from the early 1900s until about 1925.
This busy workshop would appear to be on the building's top floor. Notice the typical tailor's
cross-legged posture and the lack of sewing machines.

CASTLE FOREGATE, 1925
Looking under the Railway Bridge towards Southam's Brewery on Chester Street
during a period of severe flooding.
The site once occupied by the brewery is now the new Gateway Centre.
In the centre background, behind the man, are notices for Shrewsbury theatres.
The postcard was published by H. J. Levett of Battlefield Road.

COTON HILL, 1925

Also published by H. J. Levett showing a dry method of travel through the floods at the bottom of Coton Hill.
The open-topped charabanc, reg. no. AW 9528, was owned by Cannock House Garage of Abbey Foregate.
In the distance is the tower of the Congregational Church (built 1908/9) with the
Corporation Waterworks and Southam's Brewery on the right.

COTON HILL, c. 1909
Benbow House was built during the early 17th century and was the home of John Benbow, later
Admiral Benbow, who was born there in 1653.
At the time of this photograph, the building was used as St. Mary's Vicarage.
Today, after many alterations, it has been incorporated into garage premises.

COTON HILL, 1916

Looking up Coton Hill one sees many changes compared with the same view today.
On the left, Coton Hill cottages, which backed onto the river bank, have nearly all been
demolished. In the right foreground The London Apprentice Inn has been demolished and
replaced by another inn of the same name, but re-positioned further back from the road. The
shop on the bend, beneath the blind, was occupied by G. King, hairdresser.

CASTLE GATES, 1907

One of the many photographs, published on postcards, recording the aftermath of the major rail disaster which occured just outside the Railway Station during the early hours of 15th October, 1907. A London and North Western Railway express mail train had departed from Crewe at 1.20 a.m., later than usual. As the train approached Shrewsbury, travelling too fast, it left the tracks on a curve resulting in tragic circumstances. Several people died including three postal staff. In the centre foreground, the premises were occupied by W. Pritchard, saddle and harness maker, and S. Wood, hairdresser.

CASTLEFIELDS, 1932
This area developed from the 1830s as a self-contained community with many of its residents
employed by local industries, the canal (now drained) and the railway nearby.
Many of the houses were small. However, this imposing row of Victorian houses was built along
Severn Bank with a view looking across the meadows to Cherry Orchard.
The house at the far end was the Vicarage to All Saints' Church.

CASTLEFIELDS, c. 1912

Castle Bridge, opened in 1910, replaced a ferry which had operated for many years near to the location. The footbridge provided the shortest pedestrian route from the Railway Station to the Royal Showground via Cherry Orchard.
Notice the two signs, below and at the side of the bridge, warning about the danger of the newly built weir nearby. This footbridge was replaced in 1951 by a pre-stressed, reinforced concrete cantilever bridge; the first of its design to be built in this country.

CASTLEFIELDS

The weir was constructed across the River Severn in 1910; between Castlefields and Cherry Orchard, just below Castle Bridge.
Its construction maintained a higher level of water in the river during the summer months and so prevented the risk of falling water levels, river pollution and foul smells, which had become a major problem and health hazard in previous years.
Many local people blamed the weir as being a contributory factor to the flood disasters of later years.

CASTLE FOREGATE, 1905
At his Perseverance Iron Works, Thomas Corbett invented
many agricultural implements and machines.
On 20th November, 1905, a major fire occured which almost totally destroyed the building with
the fortunate exception of the pattern shop, which escaped the blaze.
Corbett himself narrowly missed death when a wall collapsed within the ruins as he was
surveying the damage.

ST. MICHAEL'S STREET, c. 1910

St. Michael's Church, designed by John Carline, was built in 1829-30 using yellow brick, at a total cost of £2000. It possesses an unusual tower which has two octagonal upper stages on a square base. The church was enlarged in 1855 and partially rebuilt in 1873 when the chancel was added. Sadly, St. Michael's has become one of Shrewsbury's redundant churches.

SENTINEL WORKS, 1925
At the start of World War I, most of the land north of Heathgates was open farming land.
In about 1915, the Sentinel Works in Glasgow, needing room for expansion, moved their factory to a level site beside the railway, north of Shrewsbury. The Works' output grew rapidly, producing steam waggons for the Army, and, after 1918, a wide variety of haulage vehicles. They also constructed steam railway engines, many of which possessed unusual gauges for work on foreign railways.
This postcard illustrates a Super-Sentinel articulated waggon, number 6156 (PR 5041), at the Sentinel Works. This waggon was manufactured for Bladen Farms transport, Briantspuddle, near Dorchester.

BATTLEFIELD ROAD, c. 1955

Battlefield Road was re-named Whitchurch Road in 1939. The houses on the right form part of an
estate of 100 houses erected in about 1918-19 by the Sentinel Works for its employees.
They were built in slightly curved terraces to a "garden city" plan;
an advanced and novel idea for the time.
Originally, it was intended that all hot water requirements should be provided from the Works, via the
water tower in Albert Road, but, as in many similar cases, the scheme proved to be impracticable.

ROSEWAY, HARLESCOTT, c. 1939

This Harlescott estate was constructed during the late 1930s, at a time of sporadic development in
Shrewsbury, when blocks of land were sold for the building of roads and housing.
The estate contains many houses of similar size and style, with four roads having the
prefix - Rose. The roads, Roseway, Roselyn, Rosedale and Rosemede, were formally adopted by
the Council in 1939 after their completion by the estate developers.

SUNDORNE SCHOOL, 1910

This Church of England school was capable of accommodating 88 pupils
- boys and girls - in an upper and a lower class.
In 1910, the schoolmaster was Isaac Smith and it would appear that the school was quite
well-attended and the pupils neatly dressed.
The school closed in July 1931 when the pupils were transferred to the new Harlescott Council School.

ST. MARY'S STREET, c. 1934
A fine view of the rather imposing,
imitation half-timbered frontage of
the Crown Hotel.
This building was not old by
Shrewsbury's standards,
since the original hotel was rebuilt
and enlarged c. 1908.
The 'Crown', run as a family hotel,
was finally demolished in the 1970s
to be replaced by an office and
shops complex.

ST. MARY'S STREET, c. 1932

St. Mary's Church was built on the site of an earlier Saxon Church founded by King Edgar during the late 10th century. It was rebuilt in the 12th century with many parts of its Norman architecture still remaining today. The chancel and transept were built c. 1170 and the Trinity Chapel, also known as the Draper's Chapel, in 1460. Extensive restoration was carried out towards the end of the 19th century, and also in the mid-1920s.

The 138-ft. spire, one of the tallest in England, surmounts a Norman tower holding ten bells.

The church is famous for its collection of stained glass, especially the early 14th century Jesse window in the chancel.

The cabmen's shelter, in the right foreground, was removed in 1935.

ST. MARY'S STREET, 1909

In November 1909, the Prince & Princess of Wales spent three days at Powis Castle.
Whilst the Prince went shooting, the Princess, accompanied by the Duchesses of Devonshire and Norfolk and the Countesses of Yarborough and Bradford, visited Shrewsbury and Much Wenlock.
The royal party can be seen being welcomed by the Mayor, prior to entering St. Mary's Church.

ROYAL SALOP INFIRMARY
The Infirmary started its life in a converted house in 1767.
The Salop Infirmary in St. Mary's Place was built in 1826-30 and funded by public subscription.
Gradually over the years, new sections and equipment were added including a nurses' home in 1910.
When the last patients were transferred to the new hospital in 1977,
the old Infirmary had served Shrewsbury for 210 years.

THE ENGLISH BRIDGE, 1928

The original bridge was dismantled in 1768 and a second bridge was built between 1768 and 1776 designed by J. Gwynn of Shrewsbury (see page 24). The present English Bridge was built using the dismantled Grinshill stone from the second bridge between 1925 and 1927. In August 1927, Queen Mary, whilst visitng her brother, the Marquis of Cambridge, at Shotton Hall, was driven across the almost-completed new English Bridge on her way to Whitehall (in Shrewsbury). The official opening ceremony by the Prince of Wales scheduled for 26th October, 1927, had to be cancelled at the last minute due to the death of the Marquis.
The Queen later agreed that her August drive might be designated as "the opening of the bridge".

COLEHAM HEAD, 1925
As in other parts of Shrewsbury, flooding in Coleham was a fairly regular occurrence.
Travelling through the water poses less of a problem to the man with the horse and cart than to the pedestrian.
A notice on the left warns drivers: "Danger. Overtaking on the bridge is forbidden" - a reference to the
narrowness and steep gradient of the old English Bridge.

LONGDEN COLEHAM, 1918

In August 1918, a grand Military Gymkhana took place in the School's grounds in aid of the King's
Shropshire Light Infantry Prisoners of War Fund. 5000 people attended the event.
This view of the winning Land Boat Race team is taken at the back of the Drill Hall in Coleham.
In the background can be seen the miscellany of buildings which then occupied the riverside area
on the town side of the bridge.

LONGDEN COLEHAM, 1907

The message on this postcard, dated 1st January 1907 and written from 14, Belle Vue Road, reads:
"To wish you a very happy New Year. This is our new Mission room ready for a Tea but I don't
consider it a good one of it at all and only two of the workers are there. We were too late for it.
Did Miss Y send you one of our Church. With love Catherine Evans".
It is probable that this interior view shows the Longden Coleham Mission Hall
built in 1905 by Holy Trinity Church.

2-3, ABBEY FOREGATE, c. 1922
Merivale, an L-shaped timber-framed house of handsome proportions built c. 1601, stood beside
the original Technical College (seen in the background) and later beside the Wakeman School, on
what is now school property and the entrance to the football ground.
Despite much opposition from conservationists, the house was demolished in about 1970.
Notice how the road level has altered.

ABBEY FOREGATE, c. 1912

This fête took place in Gay Meadow when much of the area formed the grounds of Merivale.
The "playing cards" were large pieces of card which were hung around necks by means of
ribbons - young children carrying the lowest numbers, whilst adults, dressed in court-style
costumes, represented the aces, kings, queens and jacks of each suit.

ABBEY FOREGATE, 1925

The Abbey was founded for the Benedictine monks by Earl Roger de Montgomery in 1083. The Church is all that remains of the great monastery. With the exception of the Refectory Pulpit, most of the monastic buildings were demolished. When the London to Holyhead road was realigned by Thomas Telford in 1836 it was built through the Abbey grounds and left the pulpit isolated. Prior to this date, the London road ran to the north of the Abbey, shown on the left of the postcard by the horses and carts. Flooding was a frequent problem in the streets surrounding the Abbey, the water often invading the Abbey itself. The postcard shows the extent of the flooding during early January 1925.

Notice the Penfold-style pillar-box by the A5 signpost. In later years, a telephone kiosk also stood at the junction by the signpost.

ABBEY FOREGATE, c. 1913
Looking towards Lord Hill's Column and showing a tranquil view of Abbey Foregate
compared with today's traffic-filled road.
Towards the Column end of Abbey Foregate, the houses lining both sides of the road were mostly
built in the late 18th and early 19th centuries, many by wealthy Shrewsbury businessmen. Most of
these spacious houses stood in extensive grounds, and today,
a number of these properties are used for local government purposes.

ABBEY FOREGATE, c. 1920
The Dun Cow Inn is thought to have become an inn during the early 1600s. It possesses a relatively uncommon carved inn sign above the porch entrance.
On the right, the premises of J. Ward, carpenter and joiner, and the houses beyond have been demolished and the site is now occupied by Safeway's store.

LORD HILL'S COLUMN, c. 1948

This magnificent monument standing at the top of Abbey Foregate commemorates Lord Rowland Hill (1772-1842) who was second in command to the Duke of Wellington at the Battle of Waterloo. The Greek Doric column, the highest in the world, was funded by public subscription and designed by Haycock (whose family was responsible for many local buildings), and built by Thomas Harrison in 1814-16. Inside the column, an iron staircase gives access to the top pedestal surmounted by the 17 feet-high statue designed by Panzetta.
In the left background, beyond the column, is St. Giles' School.

ABBEY FOREGATE

For a time The Woodlands belonged to a member of the Hazeldine family. An imposing residence with extensive grounds, it was later sold and became a boys' home.
In 1946 it became the Shrewsbury Youth Hostel.
The houses in the cul-de-sac called Woodlands Park and the section of the ring road close to the Column, constructed in the 1970s, are on land which was once part of the grounds of The Woodlands.

AERIAL VIEW, c. 1925
An early aerial view showing Abbey Foregate in the right foreground and 'Nearwell', the large house in the centre foreground, which was demolished in the 1960s to make way for the new Shirehall. This part of the town contained many substantial properties and the aerial view clearly shows the numerous changes that have occured.

WENLOCK ROAD, c. 1910

The original St. Giles' Church was connected with a leper hospital founded in the 12th century and funded by royal endowments to aid its work. Until 1836, there were only two novices per year. Between 1840 and 1863, St. Giles' was extensively rebuilt by Pountney Smith on the remains of the earlier church. When the new large houses were built in this area of Shrewsbury, St. Giles' became important to the community and it was deemed necessary to refurbish and rebuild the church.

CHERRY ORCHARD SCHOOL, 1906

The writer of this card was a Mr. Cartwright of Cherry Orchard School who ordered a "No. 9 6th Edition Time Table", and also wrote: "We have all been laid up with Influenza".
The school, for infants only, was held in the Mission Hall on the corner of Tankerville Street.
The children were probably celebrating the Coronation of King Edward VII, so that the card was used some years after the event depicted.

MONKMOOR ROAD, 1921
Whitehall was built for Richard Prince, a lawyer, in 1578-82 on land formerly belonging to the
Abbey. The building had a rich interior and this postcard shows some of the very fine panelling
and plaster work in the Drawing Room.
Whitehall owned extensive grounds,
but much of the land was sold for building purposes in the late 19th century.
At the time of this photograph, Whitehall was known as the Whitehall Hotel.

THE SHOWGROUND, MONKMOOR, 1907

Local celebrations, fêtes and the Shropshire and West Midlands Agricultural Show used to be
held on Monkmoor Showground; the site of the former Monkmoor Racecourse.
The latter opened in the early 1830s and closed for racing a decade later. The large open level
space, eventually bought by the local council, provided an ideal show site.
This postcard illustrates the large crowds watching the commencement of the parade celebrating
Empire Day in 1907. In the background are many trade stands.

THE SHOWGROUND, MONKMOOR, 1907
A close-up view of the platform for civic dignitaries shown in the centre of the previous picture.
The Mayor of Shrewsbury, Thomas Corbett, was a founder member of the Shropshire and West
Midlands Agricultural Society. He won many awards at numerous shows for his locally made
agricultural machinery.

THE SHOWGROUND, MONKMOOR, 1914

A publicity card published by Associated Portland Cement Manufacturers, London,
advertising their stand at the Royal Agricultural Society's Show held at Monkmoor Showground
in July 1914, just prior to the outbreak of World War I.
H. M. King George V visited the Show and won several awards.
He was escorted by the Mayor of Shrewsbury, Major Wingfield.
Shrewsbury has quite a number of concrete houses which date from this period. The concrete
blocks for these were manufactured in Smithfield Road.

MONKMOOR, c. 1910

In these days of heavy traffic it is difficult to imagine Monkmoor Road as a peaceful minor
country road that led past the Racecourse site to Monkmoor Farm and the old airfield.
Monkmoor Hall, built in 1840, was a large pleasant house with spacious grounds.
It was acquired by the local council and let to tenants until demolished c. 1961 for modern
housing development to take place.

BELLE VUE ROAD, 1911
The Limes stands in a very secluded situation, lying between
Longden Coleham and Belle Vue Road which was once the extent of its grounds.
Rebuilt and owned by Samuel Pountney Smith in the 1860s it has had a varied history; having
been a private residence, school, nursing home and military establishment during its life.
Pountney Smith built a number of houses in and around the Coleham area of Shrewsbury.

THE SHROPSHIRE AND MONTGOMERY RAILWAY
The Shropshire and Montgomery Railway, like the earlier ill-fated Potteries Railway, was never financially successful. Almost all of the railway stock and engines were second-hand, many items being of very unusual designs.
This tank engine, Pyramus, and a similar engine, Thisbe, were the only engines to be bought new. They were made in 1911, but proved to be too heavy for the S. & M. track.
Both engines were sold in 1914.

GALLOW'S CRAFT, MEOLE BRACE, c. 1907
Showing the dilapidated state of the track belonging to the old Potteries Railway, which ran
through Meole Brace parallel with the line to Welshpool.
On this stretch of the line, the Railway had two single platform stations; Shrewsbury West, by the
bridge on Belle Vue Road; and a station under the bridge in Meole Brace itself.
The track was improved and re-opened by the Shropshire and Montgomery Railway in 1911.

THE BRIDGE, MEOLE BRACE, c. 1908
The iron bridge, manufactured at Hazeldine's Foundry,
carried the main Hereford to Shrewsbury road across the Rea Brook at Meole Brace.
When the bypass was constructed, two new bridges had to be built; one to replace this old iron
bridge; and the second bridge to carry the new road over the railway.

MEOLE BRACE, c. 1935
The bypass was officially opened by the Princess Royal in May 1933.
The opening tape was cut at the Shelton end and the Princess Royal was then driven along the new road.
Extending from Emstrey to Shelton, the bypass was 4½ miles long with two new bridges (one shown on the postcard), four roundabouts, and with a 30 ft.-wide carriageway along its length.
The road took two years to build and cost approximately £140,000.

MEOLE BRACE, c. 1910
This is the third church to have been built in Meole Brace - the position of the second church (1799-1868) can still clearly be seen. The present church was built in 1867-88 by E. Haycock, who, like his father before him, was responsible for many buildings in Shropshire.
This church possesses possibly the finest William Morris stained glass in existence and certainly the finest Victorian stained glass in Shropshire.

MEOLE BRACE, 1906

The building of the bypass in 1933
sliced Meole Brace in two, causing
part of the village to be demolished
and effectively isolating a large area
of it to the south of the road.
The Church, Vicarage, Hall and
School lie in this latter area. For
many years members of the Bather
family were vicars of Meole Brace.
The family was responsible for the
restoration and maintenance
of the Vicarage.

MEOLE BRACE, c. 1910

The Bather family resided in Meole Brace for several generations as Lords of the Manor. They achieved a great deal of beneficial and generous work in the village, especially in building the school. Archdeacon E. Bather was responsible for the rebuilding and enlarging of the Hall; seen here with its bow window and large Victorian conservatory.

MYTTON OAK ROAD, c. 1939

Following the opening of the bypass in 1933, other roads leading off the bypass began to be laid
out and developed. Gradually, houses and estates were built as land was sold and Shrewsbury
expanded to the west and south. The hedge and two houses on the right were removed to make
way for the Copthorne shopping area and car park.

SHELTON ROAD, c. 1939

This view shows another section of the Shrewsbury bypass opened in 1933. At this end the bypass replaced a country lane. Gradually, from the late 1930s to the present decade, housing has developed along both sides of the bypass and in estates along the adjoining roads.
This card shows the section between the Copthorne and Porthill roundabouts.

THE WELSH BRIDGE, c. 1910

The medieval bridge with its gate tower survived until the 18th century.
Slightly downstream, the present Welsh Bridge, which has had many repairs over the years, was built c. 1796 to a design by Carline and Tilley, who also designed Montford Bridge. The postcard shows where the Severn could be forded (where the boys are standing) except during flood times.
On the right-hand side of the river, the buildings before the bridge were demolished when Victoria Avenue was constructed, and beyond the bridge, many properties were cleared away for the development of Raven Meadows.

FRANKWELL, 1916
Until the comparatively recent building of the dam to regulate the flow of the Severn, flooding in Frankwell was almost a "way of life" as it occurred so regularly. Residents and those wishing to go into town via the Welsh Bridge took to boats, horses, vehicles, gangplanks or simply to paddling to get through the water.
Many of the buildings seen in the background were demolished in the 20 years after World War I.

FRANKWELL, c. 1905
This view across the town was taken from Millington's Hospital and shows the crowded buildings
both in Frankwell, in the foreground, and on the town side of the Welsh Bridge.
On the skyline are the church spires, the old Market Hall, the water tower, and the tall chimney on the tannery.

THE MOUNT, c. 1938
"Beauchamp" was one of the large residences along The Mount.
When built in the late 19th century it must have been "quite out in the country" on Telford's road
to Holyhead. In 1925, a Mrs. A. E. Manford is recorded as living there, but by 1938, Mrs. A. E. Manford
had become the proprietress of "The Beauchamp Hotel" whilst residing in the adjoining house.

THE BARRACKS, 1906
The Barracks were erected along Copthorne Road between 1877-79.
The site was extensive and included all the buildings necessary to house the troops of the King's
Shropshire Light Infantry which were formed from an amalgamation of the 53rd (Shropshire)
Regiment of foot and the 80th King's Light Infantry.
The building on the left is the Orderly Room.

SHREWSBURY SCHOOL, 1931
Shrewsbury School was founded by Edward VI in 1552.
It moved from its original site, now the Library, to its new site in Kingsland in 1882.
The main building, shown on the postcard, was built as the Shrewsbury Foundling Hospital for orphans c. 1760. It later became a workhouse, and by 1824 it was occupied by 340 people. The building was acquired by the School and adapted by Sir Arthur Blomfield in 1878-82.

SHREWSBURY SCHOOL, c. 1928
An interesting and unusual view of
Shrewsbury School on its "island" site, bounded by three roads and the river.
From its beginning with one building on the new site, the School expanded gradually with
additional buildings constructed over the years. The Chapel was built to a Gothic design by
Blomfield who also designed the School House. Many of the boarding houses were erected by the
masters themselves.

SHREWSBURY SCHOOL, 1905

On 5th December, 1905, a major fire occurred at Shrewsbury School. The fire began in the upper part of the main block and quickly enveloped the roof, which, together with the bell tower and clock, collapsed into the top storeys. Boys and staff saved the valuable Library books and most of the personal possessions. Fortunately no loss of life or personal injury occurred, and by using non-teaching areas the School's academic life continued.

PORT HILL, c. 1937

The river and its bridges are very much a part of Shrewsbury's history and of its present-day life. The Port Hill Bridge, opened in 1922 and paid for mainly by the Shropshire Horticultural Society, gave easier access to the town via the Quarry. It replaced a ferry which had operated for many years from beside the Boathouse Inn. Pleasure launches and boat building also operated from this area, as advertised on W. & J. Abley's board in the centre of the picture.

ALICK LOWE & SON, c. 1914

Alick Lowe & Son, furniture remover and home furnisher, had premises on Wyle Cop.
This postcard shows Lowe's Steam traction-engine (AA 2049) and removal van.
Moving home in the early 20th century must have been a cumbersome operation and none too
kind to the furniture, judging by the way that items have been piled on top of the van, without any
covering to protect them from the weather or the smuts and soot from the traction-engine
chimney. The photograph has been identified as taken in Copthorne Road.